RAND McN

GeoTrivia SPACE

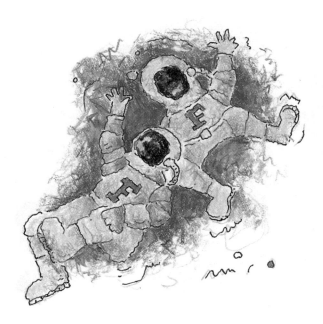

Written by Juliette Underwood   Illustrated by Susan Jacoby

Rand McNally for kids

CONTENTS

The Inside Scoop!

What's in the book?

Space Map 4

The Universe 6

The Solar System 8

The Planets 10

The Inner Planets 12

The Outer Planets 14

Asteroids, Comets, & Meteoroids 16

Stars 18

Astronomy 20

Space Travel 22

Space Exploration 24

Space Firsts 26

Astronauts 28

Space Goes to Hollywood 30

Space Challenge 32

What's on the pages?

Mind Benders

Mindbending questions—Test your knowledge, quiz your friends, and stump the grown-ups!

Answers

Correct and clever answers—Use the MINDBENDER ANSWER FLAP on the back cover to hide them. (Don't peek!)

GEO-TIP Helpful hints—Keep these handy to help you remember what's what in space!

Geo-Challenge

Experiments to test your space IQ— Take the challenge if you dare!

Top Trivia

▶ The biggest,
▶ brightest,
▶ coldest,
▶ largest,
▶ farthest space trivia ever—
  Make a quest through the "-ests"!

AMAZING FACTS

Fun and fascinating bits of information—

Amaze your friends and family with your space knowledge!

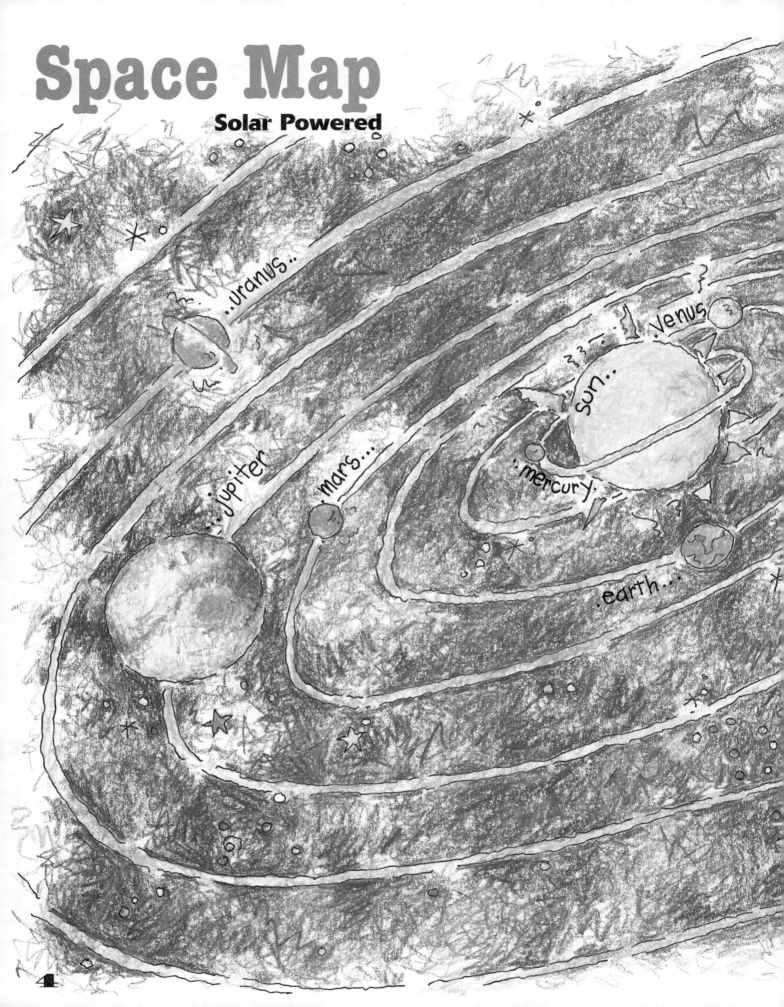

...saturn...

...neptune...

...pluto...

5

The Universe

From Here to Infinity

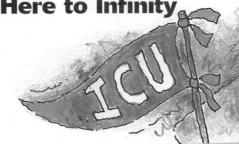

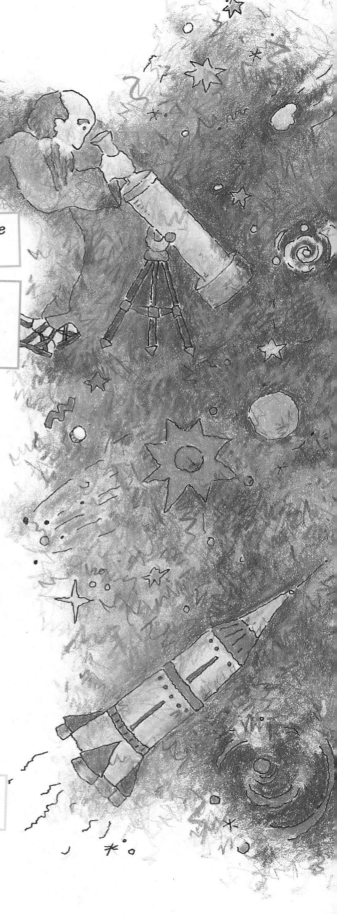

1. True or false? The universe is made up of all the galaxies and the space around them.

2. Some scientists think that the universe began with a giant explosion. What do they call that explosion? (GEO-HINT: Don't *bang* your head against the wall if you don't know the answer.)

3. The universe is enormous—it's *infinite*, but what does that mean?

4. Are galaxies and stars the same thing?

5. Choose one. How many galaxies are in the universe—hundreds, thousands, or billions?

6. Name the galaxy that our solar system is part of. (GEO-HINT: There's a famous candy bar with the same name!)

7. True or false? Galileo was the first astronomer to look at space through a telescope.

8. These collapsed stars are mysterious, can't be seen, and seem to swallow up everything around them—including light.

9. What is a "dirty snowball" that develops a long, shining tail when it comes close to the sun? (GEO-HINT: Halley's is one of the most famous in the universe.)

10. True or false? Distances in space are so great they're measured in light-years, not miles.

11. If Fred weighs 70 pounds on Earth, and Frieda weighs 60 pounds, who weighs more in space?

Answers

1. True

2. The Big Bang

3. The universe is so big that it has no boundaries—It never ends.

4. No—Galaxies are clusters of stars, planets, gas, and dust.

5. Billions (One billion is 1,000 millions!)

6. The Milky Way (Are you getting hungry?)

7. True—In the early 1600s he built his own telescope and saw craters on the moon, spots on the sun, and the four largest moons of Jupiter.

8. Black holes

9. A comet—Comets are called "dirty snowballs" because they're made of frozen gas and dust.

10. True—A light-year is the distance a beam of light travels in a year.

11. Weight a minute, that's a trick question! Neither would weigh more because they'd both be weightless.

AMAZING FACTS

The Milky Way contains millions of stars, and our sun is just one of them!

The universe is like a huge "time machine." If you look at a star in the sky that is 200 light-years away, you are actually seeing that star not as it appears today but as it appeared 200 years ago. (Better late than never, right?)

The name of our galaxy may seem strange, but some of our galaxy neighbors have even stranger names, such as Large Magellanic Cloud, Fornax dwarf, and NGC185.

The Solar System
Home Sweet Home

Mind Benders

1. What is at the center of the solar system?

2. How many planets are in the solar system?

3. Choose one. Is the sun an asteroid, a planet, or a star?

4. True or false? Without the sun we'd be alive, but very cold.

5. True or false? The sun is hottest at its center.

6. What are the dark spots on the sun's surface called?

7. True or false? Staring directly at the sun can damage your eyes and can even blind you.

8. What is the five-letter word that names the path each planet follows around the sun?

9. What is the invisible force that holds the planets in their paths around the sun? (GEO-HINT: It rhymes with *cavity*.)

10. This happens when the moon passes directly between Earth and the sun and blocks the sun's light.

11. Is the moon a planet?

12. Choose one. Which of these is NOT a phase of the moon—a new moon, a blue moon, or a full moon?

13. True or false? Like the sun, the moon gives off its own light.

Geo-Challenge

Compared to the moon, the sun is gigantic. So how can the moon cover the sun during a solar eclipse?

Look at a large object that's far away. Close one eye and hold your fist in front of the open eye. Even though it's smaller, your fist covers the object.

The moon is like your fist. It's smaller, but closer. Because of that, the moon is large enough to cover the sun.

AMAZING FACTS

A long time ago, people were afraid of solar eclipses (when the moon blocks the sun's light). They thought eclipses were dragons in the sky trying to eat the sun. People would yell, blow horns, and stamp their feet to scare the dragon away. It worked every time!

If you could walk for 100 years, day and night without stopping, you would make it around the sun only one time!

If the sun were a giant gumball machine, it would take more than one million gumballs the size of Earth to fill it.

Answers

1. The sun

2. Nine (That we know of!)

3. A star—Think of this "star" as "taking center stage" in our solar system.

4. False—Without the sun there wouldn't be any life on Earth.

5. True—That's where the sun makes its heat and light energy.

6. Sunspots—These "freckles" on the sun look darker because they are cooler than the rest of the sun's surface.

7. True (Just ask the famous astronomer Galileo. He damaged his eyes by looking at the sun through his telescope.)

8. O-R-B-I-T

9. Gravity (The same force that keeps you glued to your seat as you read this book!)

10. A solar eclipse (But how can the moon block the sun when the moon is so much smaller? Check out GEO-CHALLENGE.)

11. No—The moon is a satellite that orbits the planet Earth.

12. A blue moon (Although there is a saying, once in a blue moon, which means "hardly ever.")

13. False—The moon steals light from the sun and reflects it back to us on Earth.

The Planets
Spheres in Space

1. Name the planets, in order, starting with the planet that is closest to the sun.

2. True or false? All of the planets travel around the sun in the same direction.

3. Can you name the biggest and the smallest planets?

4. Which planet is the hottest?

5. Name at least two of the four planets that do NOT have solid surfaces. (GEO-HINT: They are all "outer planets.")

6. This planet looks like it's tipped sideways.

7. The Great Red Spot is found on which planet?

8. This planet is often called the "red planet."

9. True or false? All of the planets have moons.

10. Which planets have plants and animals?

11. Name the blue planets.

12. Which planet has the most moons? (GEO-HINT: It's also known for its beautiful rings.)

Top Trivia

▶ Did you think Pluto was the planet farthest from the sun? Most of the time it is, but sometimes it sneaks inside Neptune's orbit. Until 1999, Neptune is actually farthest from the sun.

▶ Jupiter is so gigantic that 1,300 Earths could fit inside it.

GEO-TIP Use this wacky sentence to help you remember the planets in order: *Must Vera Eat MARShmallow and Jelly Sandwiches Under Ned's Porch?*

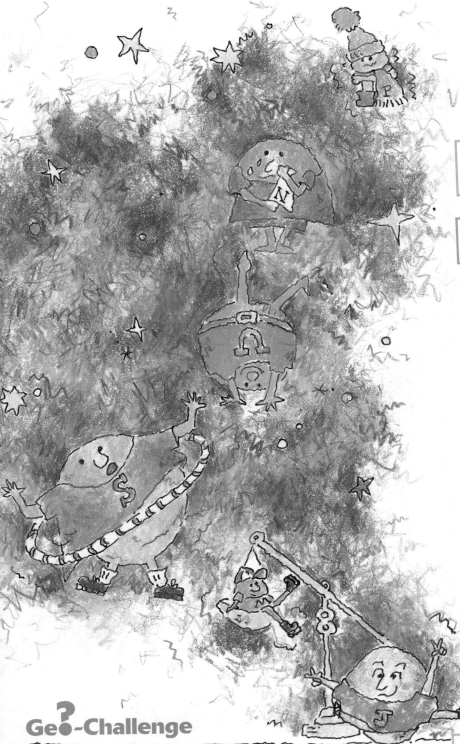

Geo-Challenge

If you weighed 70 lbs. on Earth, you'd tip the scales at a slender 19 lbs. on Mercury but a whopping 185 lbs. on Jupiter. (No weigh!) Figure out what you'd weigh on these planets by using the following equations. (You might need a calculator!)

your weight × 0.27 = Mercury weight

your weight × 2.64 = Jupiter weight

Answers

1. Mercury, Venus, Earth, Mars, Jupiter, Saturn, Uranus, Neptune, Pluto

2. True

3. Jupiter is the biggest, and Pluto is the smallest. (Pluto is also the coldest.)

4. Venus—The clouds that cover Venus hold in the heat, making it hotter than an oven.

5. Jupiter, Saturn, Uranus, Neptune

6. Uranus—This tipped position causes Uranus to have 42 years of sunlight followed by 42 years of darkness. (Yikes!)

7. Jupiter

8. Mars—The rust in its soil makes it look red.

9. False—Mercury and Venus are moonless.

10. Trick question! Only one—Earth (As far as we know!)

11. Uranus and Neptune—They look blue because of the methane gas in their atmosphere.

12. Saturn—It has more than 20 moons.

The Inner Planets
On the Inside Track

Mind Benders

1. Name the inner planets.

2. Why are they called the "inner planets"?

3. Are the surfaces of the inner planets made up of rocks or gases?

4. True or false? Since Mercury is closest to the sun, it is the hottest planet.

5. This planet is the only one with liquid water on its surface.

6. At one time, people thought there might be life on this planet. (GEO-HINT: They thought "little green men" lived there.)

7. True or false? The largest volcano in the solar system is on Earth.

8. Which two inner planets are called the "sister planets" because they're almost the same size?

9. This planet is the only one that rotates from east to west—all other planets rotate from west to east.

10. This planet has the largest canyon in the solar system.

11. Which is the smallest inner planet? (GEO-HINT: It's also the speediest planet in its orbit around the sun.)

Planet or space ship?

little green men and lava

AMAZING FACTS

If you lived on our moon, you could yell and scream as much as you'd like. There's no air to carry sound!

Mars has two tiny moons, Phobos and Deimos, which look like a pair of lumpy potatoes. Some scientists think that Phobos will eventually crash into Mars, but not for many millions of years. (Talk about mashed potatoes!)

Top Trivia

▶ *Venus is the brightest planet. It's so bright that people have mistaken it for a UFO.*

▶ *Since it orbits the sun so fast, Mercury holds the record for the shortest year in the solar system—88 days. Birthdays would roll around pretty quickly on Mercury—4 birthdays on Mercury for every 1 birthday on Earth!*

the party planet

which planet can you see most often without a telescope?

earth!

the big drip

Answers

1. Mercury, Venus, Earth, Mars

2. They're the ones closest to the sun. (Like the inside lanes of a race track!)

3. Rocks—These planets are also known as the "terrestrial planets." (*Terrestrial* means "land.")

4. Sounds true, but it's false—Venus is the hottest planet.

5. Earth—We need that water to stay alive.

6. Mars—Those "little green men" were known as Martians.

7. False—The largest volcano is *Olympus Mons,* a huge volcano on Mars. It's 16 miles, or almost 26 kilometers, high!

8. Venus and Earth—These two planets are neighbors, too, which is another reason they're called the "sister planets."

9. Venus—That means the sun rises in the *west* and sets in the *east* on Venus. (Is your head spinning from all this information?)

10. Mars—The canyon is 13 times longer and 4 times deeper than the Grand Canyon.

11. Quick, did you answer Mercury? (Mercury was named after the speediest messenger of the Roman gods.)

THE OUTER PLANETS

The Outer Limits

1. How many outer planets are there? Can you name them?

2. Name the only outer planet that is not made up of gases. (GEO-HINT: This one's way out there!)

3. How many of the outer planets have moons?

4. True or false? All of the outer planets have rings.

5. Only this planet's rings can be seen through a telescope from Earth.

6. Choose one. Is the Great Red Spot on Jupiter a storm, a volcano, or a crater?

7. True or false? Neptune has a Great Dark Spot, which is like Jupiter's Great Red Spot.

8. Choose one. Are the rings around Saturn made mostly of beautiful rays of light, chunks of ice and rock, or poofs of sparkles and smoke?

9. True or false? Some astronomers think that Uranus is tipped sideways because a huge object smashed into it after it was formed.

10. Which planet was hit by a comet in 1994?

11. Do astronomers believe that there's a planet beyond Pluto in our solar system?

Top Trivia

▶ *Pluto has the longest year in the solar system. It takes Pluto about 248 years to orbit the sun. Imagine waiting 248 years to celebrate your birthday!*

▶ *Jupiter wins the prize for the planet with the shortest day—about 10 hours. That would mean you'd only have time for 2 1/2 hours of school and 3 hours of sleep. (Sounds pretty good, huh?) But how much time would you have to play, eat, and watch TV? (WHOA! A 24-hour day isn't so bad after all.)*

▶ *Things are pretty chilly on Triton, Neptune's largest moon. With a temperature of −390° F (−234° C), scientists believe that Triton is the coldest place in the solar system!*

1. Five—Jupiter, Saturn, Uranus, Neptune, Pluto

2. Pluto—It's made up of rock and ice.

3. All of them—They range in number from 1 (Pluto) to more than 20 (Saturn).

4. False—All of the outer planets except Pluto have rings.

5. Saturn's—We didn't know about the other planets' rings until space vehicles called probes discovered them.

6. A huge storm—It's actually the largest hurricane in the solar system, measuring almost three times the size of Earth.

7. True

8. Chunks of ice and rock—Some pieces are as tiny as grains of sand, while other pieces are as big as houses!

9. True (This poor planet doesn't know which end is up!)

10. Jumpin' Jupiter!—A string of 21 fragments from the comet Shoemaker-Levy 9 struck Jupiter during the week of July 16, 1994.

11. Yes and no—Some astronomers think that there is a "Planet X" beyond Pluto. Others think it's unlikely.

CAUTION FALLING ROCKS

THIS EXIT INNER PLANETS

ASTEROIDS, COMETS & METEOROIDS
Rocks in Space

1. Choose one. Are asteroids, comets, or meteoroids sometimes known as "minor planets"?

2. Are asteroids mostly round like planets, or are they all different shapes?

3. Some astronomers think that this planet is so small it should be considered an asteroid.

4. Choose one. What's the name of the group of asteroids found between Mars and Jupiter—the planet belt, the asteroid belt, or the black belt?

5. True or false? Asteroids that pass close to Earth are called "Earth-grazers."

6. True or false? Because comets are a mixture of frozen gas and rock dust, they're sometimes called "dirty dustballs."

7. When a comet orbits close to the sun, does the comet disappear or grow a long tail?

8. Choose one. Does Halley's comet, one of the most famous comets, appear every 2 years, 10 years, or 76 years?

9. What do you call a meteoroid that travels through Earth's atmosphere and hits the ground? (GEO-HINT: It rhymes with satellite.)

10. True or false? Falling stars and shooting stars are not really stars at all—they're meteors.

11. You won't get wet with this kind of shower.

12. Was Jupiter hit by a gigantic asteroid, an exploding comet, or a burning meteoroid in 1994?

GEO-TIP *What's the difference?*

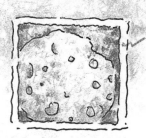

METEOROIDS *are fragments of rock that orbit the sun.*

AMAZING FACTS

Long ago, people thought a comet was a warning sign for war because a comet's long tail looked like a knife or sword.

Some scientists believe that the dinosaurs became extinct when a huge comet or asteroid slammed into Earth.

Mark Twain, who wrote about Huckleberry Finn and Tom Sawyer, was born and died on days when Halley's comet could be seen on Earth.

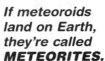

*They burn up in streaks of light called **METEORS** when they enter Earth's atmosphere.*

*If meteoroids land on Earth, they're called **METEORITES**.*

Answers

1. Asteroids (As a matter of fact, the largest asteroid, Ceres, was once considered a planet.)

2. All different shapes—Some are shaped like bricks, potatoes, or mountains. (There's even one, called Hector, that's shaped like a dumbbell!)

3. Pluto (They think Pluto's moon, Charon, should be considered an asteroid, too.)

4. The asteroid belt, which is made up of about 40,000 asteroids

5. True

6. False—They're called "dirty snowballs."

7. It grows a long tail—The yellowish part of that tail is made of dust, and the bluish part is made of gas. (Did you know the word *comet* means "long-haired star"?)

8. About every 76 years—It was last seen in 1986.

9. You were quite right if you said meteorite!

10. True—When meteoroids enter Earth's atmosphere they sometimes burn up in streaks of light called meteors.

11. A meteor shower!

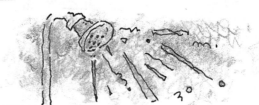

12. An exploding comet

Stars

Starlight, Stars Bright

1. Is a star a glowing ball of hot gas, a streak of light, or a famous person?

2. True or false? Stars twinkle because their lights turn on and off.

3. Are all stars the same color?

4. Choose one. Which of these is NOT a kind of star—a red giant, a green giant, or a white dwarf?

5. Do stars live forever?

6. True or false? Smaller stars live longer than larger ones.

7. Are exploding stars called shooting stars or supernovas?

8. What do you call a group of stars that looks like a picture in the sky?

9. Many stars have names. What's the name of the star directly above the North Pole?

10. Do the constellations Taurus, Cancer, Leo, and Aries look like animals, cars, or people?

11. Is one of the most famous clusters of stars the Seven Sisters or the Seven Dwarfs?

Geo-Challenge

Can you find the North Star?

Locate the Big Dipper (have a grown-up help you, if necessary). Then trace an imaginary line up from the bottom star of the dipper end to the top star.

Keep tracing straight up and you'll find the North Star—every time!

AMAZING FACTS

Stars have cool patches, or spots, just like the sun, but instead of sunspots, they're called *starspots*.

What's the longest word you can think of? Whatever it is, it probably doesn't even come close to the name of the star *Shurnarkabtishashutu*. (Just try to say that three times fast!)

A constellation looks like a huge connect-the-dots picture in the sky. The stars that make up that picture appear close to one another, but they are actually millions of miles apart.

Answers

1. A glowing ball of hot gas (Well, the answer *could* be a famous person, but this is a book about space!)

2. False—Stars only *look* like they twinkle because their light gets bent and shifted as it passes through Earth's atmosphere. (Maybe that song should be "Crinkle, Crinkle, Little Star"!)

3. No—Stars come in a rainbow of colors, depending on their temperature.

4. A green giant is not a kind of star.

5. No—Stars are born and die, but they live for billions of years. Nearly 20 new stars are born in our galaxy each year.

6. True

7. Supernovas—This can happen when some of the largest stars die.

8. A constellation

9. The North Star—Sailors have used this star to guide them for thousands of years.

10. Animals (Although Taurus and Aries are car names!)

11. The Seven Sisters—This star cluster is in the constellation of Taurus.

Astronomy
The Study of the Stars and Beyond

1. True or false? Astronomy is the newest science.

2. Do astronomers study stars and planets or astrodomes and astroturf?

3. If a *stellar* astronomer studies the stars, what does a *solar* astronomer study?

4. What "windy city" has the first planetarium ever built in the western hemisphere?

5. Who was the first astronomer to say that the planets travel around the sun, rather than around Earth—Copernicus or Newton?

6. True or false? Halley was the first astronomer to study the skies through a telescope.

7. Maria Mitchell, the first female astronomer in the United States, has a crater named after her. Is the crater on Mars or on the moon?

8. What do modern astronomers use radio telescopes for—getting clearer signals on their radios or listening to radio waves from space?

9. Why are most observatories (buildings that hold giant telescopes) built on mountains instead of in valleys?

10. True or false? The telescopes in observatories rotate at the same speed as Earth so that they can follow objects in the sky.

11. When astronomer Jocelyn Bell first discovered pulsars, she called them LGM. Does LGM stand for "Light Green Meteorites" or "Little Green Men"?

Top Trivia

▶ Astronomer Carolyn Shoemaker has discovered 28 comets so far—more than anyone else in the world! Her most famous discovery was the Shoemaker-Levy 9 comet that crashed into Jupiter in 1994. (She co-discovered the comet with her husband, Eugene, and David Levy.)

▶ Pluto is the most recently discovered planet in our solar system. In 1930, Clyde Tombaugh was using a microscope to compare detailed photographs of star images when he detected Pluto.

Answers

1. False—It's one of the oldest sciences.

2. Stars and planets (And everything else in the universe!)

3. The sun (There are also other kinds of astronomers, like observational, planetary, and theoretical astronomers.)

4. Chicago, home of the Adler Planetarium

5. Copernicus (And boy, did he get into trouble for it!)

6. False—It was Galileo. (He made that telescope himself.)

7. The moon

8. Listening to radio waves from space

9. The air is much clearer and the sky is much darker high in the mountains.

10. True

11. "Little Green Men"—Bell thought the radio waves from the pulsars might have been coming from beings in space. But pulsars are really neutron stars that give off pulses of light and radio waves.

AMAZING FACTS

Using a radio telescope, astronomers discovered "quasi-stellar," or somewhat star-like, objects that they think are the middles of very young galaxies. These bright but distant objects are called "quasars."

Some people think that Stonehenge, a circle of huge stones in England, might have been used in ancient times to keep track of the sun's movements.

Astronomer Percival Lowell built the Lowell Observatory in Flagstaff, Arizona, so he could study the surface of Mars. He believed there were canals on Mars' surface that were built by intelligent beings.

SPACE TRAVEL
Up, Up, and Away!

1. NASA was formed to study space and space flight. Do you know what NASA stands for?

2. You hear "10. . .9. . .8. . ." during every rocket launch. What is this part of the launch called?

3. True or false? Mercury, Gemini, and Apollo are the names of different types of spacecraft.

4. How many crew, or people, could fit inside the Gemini spacecraft—1, 2, or 8?

5. What was the goal of the Apollo missions?

6. How many Americans walked on the moon during the Apollo missions—12, 32, or 50?

7. Where did the Mercury, Gemini, and Apollo spacecraft land? (GEO-HINT: These missions ended in a splashdown.)

8. In 1986, Russia sent up Mir, the first permanent space station. Does Mir mean "star," "sky," or "peace"?

9. True or false? A space shuttle is a spacecraft that can be used only once.

10. All space shuttles are launched from the Kennedy Space Center in this state.

11. Do space shuttles splash down?

12. Which is NOT a goal of space shuttle journeys—to carry satellites into orbit, to perform experiments, or to visit other planets?

13. True or false? Scientists are working on an idea for a spacecraft called a "solar sail," which would catch sunlight and use it to sail through the solar system.

Geo-Challenge

Do you understand how rockets work? When the fuel inside a rocket burns, it turns into very hot gas. That gas shoots out of the rocket and makes it move forward.

To see how a rocket works, blow up a balloon and let it go. Think of your breath as the balloon's fuel—its "hot gas." As the hot gas shoots out, the balloon shoots forward.

AMAZING FACTS

Have you ever seen a UFO? Astronaut James McDivitt thought he did. According to McDivitt, there was some kind of object with arms sticking out of it, passing about 9½ miles away from his space capsule.

Pollution is even a problem in space! The amount of "space junk"—old spacecraft and exploded rockets—increases after every rocket launch. Thousands of pieces of debris orbit Earth.

Answers

1. National Aeronautics and Space Administration

2. The countdown

3. True

4. Two (And boy was it crowded! Today's space shuttles carry seven astronauts comfortably.)

5. To reach the moon

6. Twelve lucky Americans! (But no one has walked on the moon since 1972.)

7. In the sea—The astronauts were then picked up by the recovery team helicopter.

8. "Peace"—This space station is supposed to remain in space until the end of the century.

9. False—A space shuttle can be used over and over. (Wow, talk about recycling!)

10. Florida—Spacecraft launched near the equator in Florida get an extra "push" because the Earth spins faster there.

11. No—Space shuttles land on a runway like airplanes.

12. To visit other planets (Not yet, anyway!)

13. True (Cool—solar surfing!)

...gemini...

...mir...

...mercury...

10... 9... 8...

Space Exploration

Is Anybody Out There?

1. True or false? A satellite is an object that orbits, or moves around, another object in space.

2. The "space age" began in 1957 when this country launched a satellite called *Sputnik 1* into space.

3. True or false? Before *Sputnik 1* was launched into orbit, the moon was Earth's only satellite.

4. Is a space probe an unmanned exploration craft or a space station?

5. Every planet except this one has been explored by space probes.

6. Which object in space has been explored more than any other?

7. True or false? Just in case there are other beings in space, the *Voyager* probes carry messages about Earth.

8. Eleven space probes have landed on Venus. How long did most of them last before burning up—less than 2 hours, less than 2 days, or less than 2 weeks?

9. The world's first space telescope, or "observatory in the sky," was launched in 1990. Can you name it?

10. That first space telescope has had some problems that needed fixing. Was one of them blurry vision, a noisy muffler, or a broken radio?

11. True or false? Satellites and telescopes sometimes "hitch a ride" into space on space shuttles.

GEO-TIP *Do you know the difference?*

NATURAL SATELLITES *are heavenly bodies that orbit around other heavenly bodies. Our moon and all the other planets' moons are natural satellites.*

The Russian probe *Luna 3* photographed the moon in 1959, giving scientists their first glimpse of the far side of the moon.

Satellites aren't just used for studying the universe. There are weather satellites, communications satellites, and even spy satellites! Satellites help us make long-distance phone calls and bring us television programs from around the world.

The Hubble Space Telescope is so powerful that if you looked through it on Earth, you would be able to see a penny from about 435 miles away!

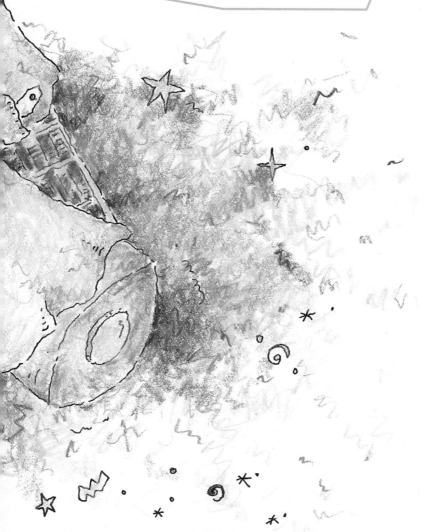

ARTIFICIAL SATELLITES are objects that have been made and sent into orbit by people here on Earth.

Answers

1. True (Do you know the difference between natural and artificial satellites? If not, check out GEO-TIP.)

2. The Soviet Union

3. True—It was Earth's only satellite for billions of years.

4. An unmanned exploration craft (Probes take pictures and send information back to Earth for scientists to study.)

5. Pluto (Probes have actually landed on Venus and Mars.)

6. The Earth's moon (The moon has been explored by space probes and by people.)

7. True (They carry phonograph records with sounds of crickets, volcanoes, laughter, a jet plane, Morse code, and a kiss!)

8. Less than two hours

9. The Hubble Space Telescope

10. Blurry vision—But it was corrected in 1994 with a new set of "contact lenses."

11. True

Space Firsts

Beat You to It!

1. The very first earthling to go into space was an animal. Do you know what kind of animal it was?

2. The first person to go into space was Yuri Gagarin. What country was he from? (GEO-HINT: In Yuri's country, he was called a *cosmonaut*.)

3. The first American to go into space was Alan Shepard. How long did his flight last— 15 minutes, 15 hours, or 15 days?

4. John Glenn was the first astronaut to eat in space. Did he eat ice cream, applesauce, or space food sticks?

5. Who was the first American woman in space— Sally Ride or Mae Jemison?

6. During which mission did Neil Armstrong and Edwin Aldrin become the first men to walk on the moon—*Vostok 6, Gemini 4,* or *Apollo 11?*

7. True or false? When Neil Armstrong first stepped onto the moon, he said, "That's one small step for a man because I've got one small foot."

8. What was the first thing Armstrong did after stepping on the moon—stuff moon rocks into his pockets, take pictures, or look for a bathroom?

9. True or false? Edward H. White, the first American to walk in space, was having so much fun that his commander had to tell him to get back into the spacecraft.

10. Did Svetlana Savitskaya become the first woman to walk in space in 1964, 1974, or 1984?

11. In February 1995, the *Discovery* space shuttle journey had lots of famous firsts. Can you name one?

The race is on!

SPACE RACE

...to be continued...

1990

1973

1971

1969

Answers

1. No, it wasn't the cow that jumped over the moon! It was a dog named Laika.

2. The Soviet Union—Gagarin orbited the Earth once and then came home again—all in 108 minutes.

3. Fifteen minutes (It's still the shortest space flight on record!)

4. Applesauce—He squeezed it out of a tube and into his mouth.

5. Sally Ride (Mae Jemison was the first African-American woman in space.)

6. *Apollo 11*

7. False (What he *really* said was, "That's one small step for a man, one giant leap for mankind.")

8. He stuffed moon rocks into his pockets.

9. True

10. 1984 (19 years after the first man walked in space!)

11. Eileen Collins was the first female pilot, Bernard Harris became the first African American to walk in space, and the *Discovery* crew members tested new space suits—To name a few!

AMAZING FACTS

In 1984, Bruce McCandless was the first astronaut to use the Manned Maneuvering Unit (MMU), a self-propelling backpack that allowed him to fly untethered in space.

In 1971, Apollo 15 astronauts drove their first "space car" on the moon. The car, called a "Lunar Rover," carried the astronauts a little over 17 miles and was the first of 3 rovers that U.S. astronauts left behind on the moon.

Skylab, the first U.S. space station, was launched in 1973 and was living and working quarters for three crews of astronauts. *Skylab's* plunge back to Earth in 1979 caused quite a stir—no one knew exactly where it would fall. (Look out below!)

ASTRONAUTS
Pioneers in Space

Mind Benders

1. True or false? The word astronaut means "hiker among the stars."

2. True or false? Mission specialists, payload specialists, and pilots are all different kinds of astronauts.

3. There is none of this in space, so astronauts don't weigh anything up there.

4. Do astronauts practice in a pool of water, jelly, or mud to learn how to float in space?

5. When space travel began, it took astronauts about an hour to get into their space suits. How long does it take them now—5 seconds, 5 minutes, or 5 hours?

6. Do astronauts have to wear space suits all the time in space?

7. When astronauts cry in space, where do their tears go?

8. After astronauts brush their teeth, what do they do with the toothpaste in their mouths? (GEO-HINT: They can't spit it out—it will float away!)

9. What are astronauts NOT able to do inside a spacecraft—run, float, or glide?

10. Do astronauts play with toys in space?

11. True or false? Almost anyone can be an astronaut.

12. If you and your friends wanted to find out what it's like to be an astronaut, you could go to this kind of camp.

Geo-Challenge

Try this to understand the challenge of eating and drinking in space:

Put a glass of water on the floor next to a chair. Lie across the chair and let your head hang lower than your stomach. Try to drink out of the glass.

It's not easy, is it? You don't have gravity to help pull the water down your throat and through your body!

Now try drinking with the straw. Does the straw help?

28

AMAZING FACTS

Space walking can be dangerous! Astronauts carry puncture repair kits to patch up holes they might get in their space suits from flying meteoroids.

Astronauts' bodies change in space. The fluid in their lower bodies moves up, so their legs and waists get skinnier. And since gravity doesn't push down on their backbones, they grow an inch or two.

How do astronauts "lie down" when they are sleeping? They strap themselves into sleeping bags that are attached to a stable surface. But if arms aren't tucked in, they won't stay at an astronaut's sides—they'll rise in the air!

Answers

1. False—It means "sailor among the stars."

2. True—They each have different jobs in space.

3. Gravity (To train for the feeling caused by zero gravity, some astronauts train in an aircraft nicknamed the "Vomit Comet.")

4. Water (Moving underwater is the closest thing to feeling weightless.)

5. Five minutes

6. No—On the space shuttle, the living quarters and work areas have air, so astronauts can wear normal clothing there.

7. They float all around. (Just like everything else in space!)

8. They swallow it—YUK!—or spit it into a towel.

9. Run (However, astronauts are able to use specially adapted treadmills and exercycles.)

10. Yes, they do! (Astronauts have played with yo-yos, jacks, and marbles to see how they work in space.)

11. False—Astronauts have to be in excellent health; work well in groups and under stress; and have a college degree in math, meteorology, astronomy, physics, computers, biology, or geology.

12. Space camp (One popular camp is at The Space and Rocket Center in Huntsville, Alabama.)

Space Goes to Hollywood

The Stars are Really Stars

1. Choose one. In the TV show *Star Trek*, what was the name of the starship that carried the crew through space—*Entertainer, Enterprise,* or *Enter Laughing?*

2. True or false? The crew's mission was to "boldly go where no one else really wanted to go."

3. The original crew of *Star Trek* had one member who was not from Earth. Who was he? (GEO-HINT: He was the logical Vulcan with the pointy ears.)

4. When the Death Star blew up in *Star Wars* and again in *Return of the Jedi*, it exploded in a gigantic firestorm. Is this *really* possible in space?

5. In the movie *The Empire Strikes Back*, did Luke Skywalker find out that Darth Vader was his cousin, his uncle, or his father?

6. Choose one. In the movie *E.T.*, what did E.T. want to do—go home, order a pizza, or take a bike ride?

7. What does *E.T.* stand for?

8. What Earth food did E.T. love to eat—candy, popcorn, or ice cream?

9. In the TV show *The Honeymooners*, where in the solar system did Ralph Kramden want to send his wife, Alice? (GEO-HINT: The answer is hidden in the show's name.)

10. In what TV show did astronaut Tony Nelson find a genie in a bottle after a splashdown?

11. In the TV cartoon *The Jetsons*, what was the name of the family dog?

Geo-Challenge

Can you think of words or phrases that have to do with space? (How about "far out!," "spacey," "space cadet," "starry-eyed," "stellar," "solar," and "universal"?)

Try keeping a list for one week of all the "space" words and phrases you hear. Share them with your friends and see if they can tell you what the words mean or where they come from.

Answers

1. Enterprise (The *U.S.S. Enterprise*, to be exact!)

2. False—They wanted to "boldly go where no man has gone before."

3. Spock (His father was from Vulcan, and his mother was from Earth.)

4. No—There is no air in space. (Remember, fire needs air to burn.)

5. His father

6. Go home (He tried to phone home to tell them where he was.)

7. Extra-Terrestrial

8. Candy (Do you remember what kind it was?)

9. "To the moon, Alice!" was Ralph's familiar cry.

10. *I Dream of Jeannie*

11. Astro (Or "Rastro," as Astro would say!)

AMAZING FACTS

In 1938, *War of the Worlds*, a radio play about an invasion, was so convincing that many listeners thought it was an actual report. They thought Martians had invaded New Jersey!

Remember the Imperial Snowwalkers in *The Empire Strikes Back*? They looked huge, didn't they? In real life they were only 18 inches high, and the way they moved was modeled after an elephant's walk.

R2-D2 from the movie *Star Wars* was played by 38-inch-tall actor Kenny Baker. When he got tired of standing in his costume, he sat down inside of it! But actor Anthony Daniels, who played C-3PO, could never sit down. His costume was so stiff he could only relax by leaning against a board.

SPACE CHALLENGE
Picture This!

What's wrong with this picture? Find 10 things that just *can't* be true.

1. Space shuttles don't splash down!   2. You can scream on the moon, but no one will hear you.   3. Never look directly at the sun!   4. Astronauts must wear space suits outside the spacecraft, and they can't run in space.   5. A house, or any other object, would burn up pretty quickly on Venus—it's too hot!   6. Observatories are on mountain tops, not in valleys.   7. Mercury is moonless.   8. The Great Red Spot is on Jupiter, not Mars.   9. It's a countdown, not a countup!   10. The first animal in space was a dog, not a monkey.